Little Christmas Joys
LINEWORK PATTERN WORKBOOK
by Annie Lang

You can share the memories and spread the Christmas Joy this holiday season with all the festive characters you'll find within the pages of this pattern publication. Choose from dozens of mix and match themed character designs created from Annie's Christmas Kids, Holiday Penguins, Holiday Mice and Roly Poly Holidays collection of images.

Simply trace the design and then transfer the image onto your project surface to make outstanding personalized items with professional results every time.

Transferring the linework designs

Trace the design of your choice with pencil and tracing paper. Place transfer paper under the tracing paper and place onto your selected surface. Hold in place with tape if necessary. Retrace over the linework to transfer the design onto the project. For fabrics, trace the design, flip the pattern over and retrace the lines using a fabric transfer pen. Follow manufacturer's direction to iron the design onto your chosen fabric item.

Color or paint these designs with

Craft paints, watercolors, markers, coloring pencils, chalks, inks, fabric pens, paint pens, or crayons

These designs are great for

Home Dec Items like furniture, cabinets, accent items, walls, lamps, glassware, kitchen accessories, office and desk items, bathroom accents, cabinets, patio pots and outdoor items, etc.
Fabric and wearable items like t-shirts, sweatshirts, aprons, canvas shoes, totes, quilting squares, table linens and napkins, window and shower curtains, pillows, etc.
Paper Craft Projects like greeting cards, scrap page elements, tags, labels, stationery items, ornaments, gift bags, etc.

For more ideas and designer tips, please visit my Blog at

http://annielang-anniethingspossible.blogspot.com/
My Pinterest Board at http://www.pinterest.com/anniethings/
or my Facebook Page at
http://www.facebook.com/anniethingspossible

anniethingspossible.com
creative designs by Annie Lang

Roly Poly Holidays

Annie's Holiday Helper Kids

Copyright (C) Annie Lang
www.anniethingspossible.com

FRAGILE
HANDLE
WITH CARE

OUR
FAVORITE
ORNAMENTS

repeatable border design

Annie's
Singing
Christmas Mice

'tis the season to be JOLLY!

'tis the season to be JOLLY!

Roly Poly
Holidays

Copyright (C)
Annie Lang
www.anniethingspossible.com

HOLIDAY PENGUINS

HOLIDAY PENGUINS

HOLIDAY PENGUINS

HOLIDAY PENGUINS

HOLIDAY PENGUINS

HOLIDAY PENGUINS

Copyright (C) Annie Lang
www.anniethingspossible.com

HOLIDAY PENGUINS

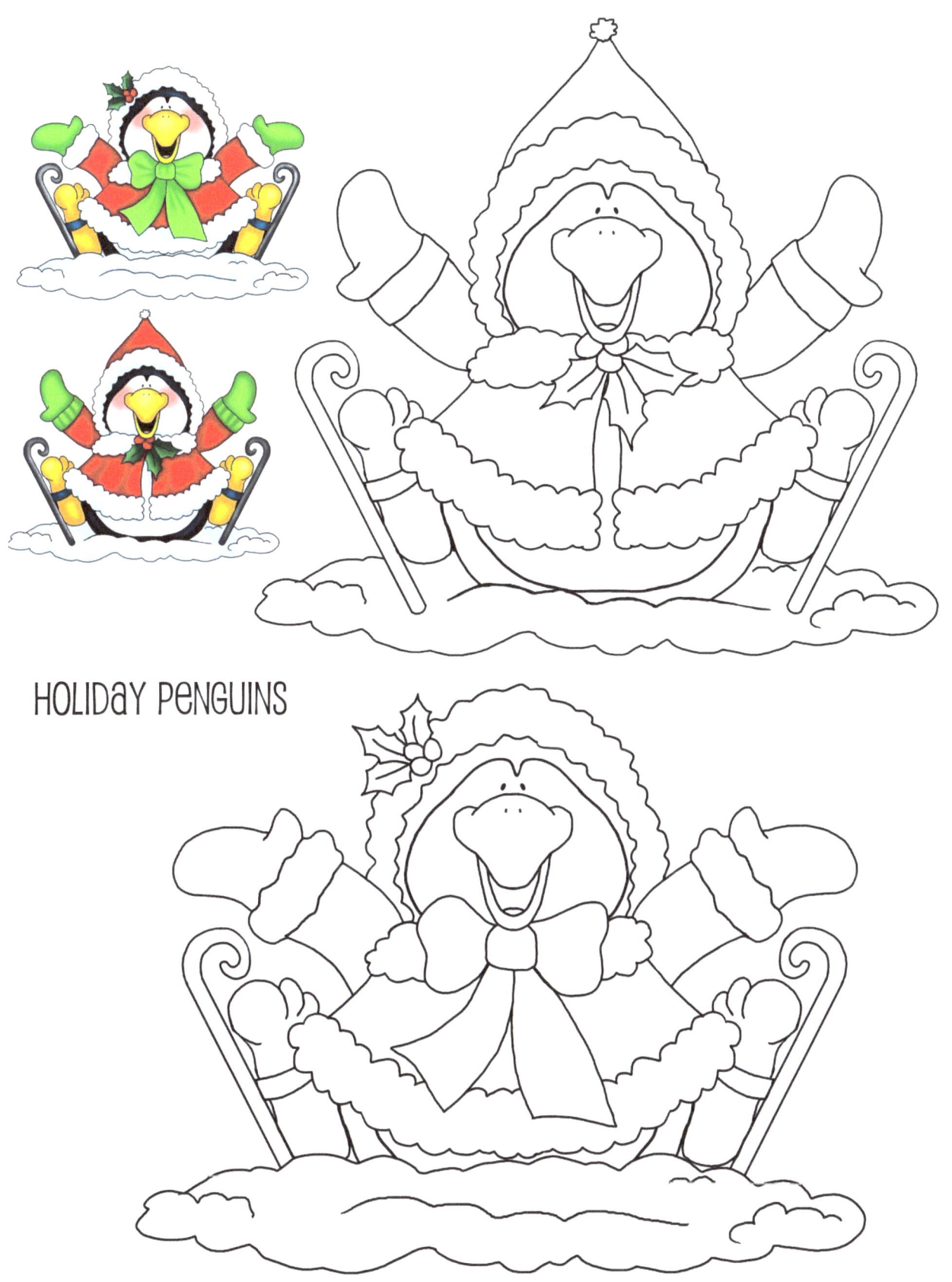

HOLIDAY PENGUINS

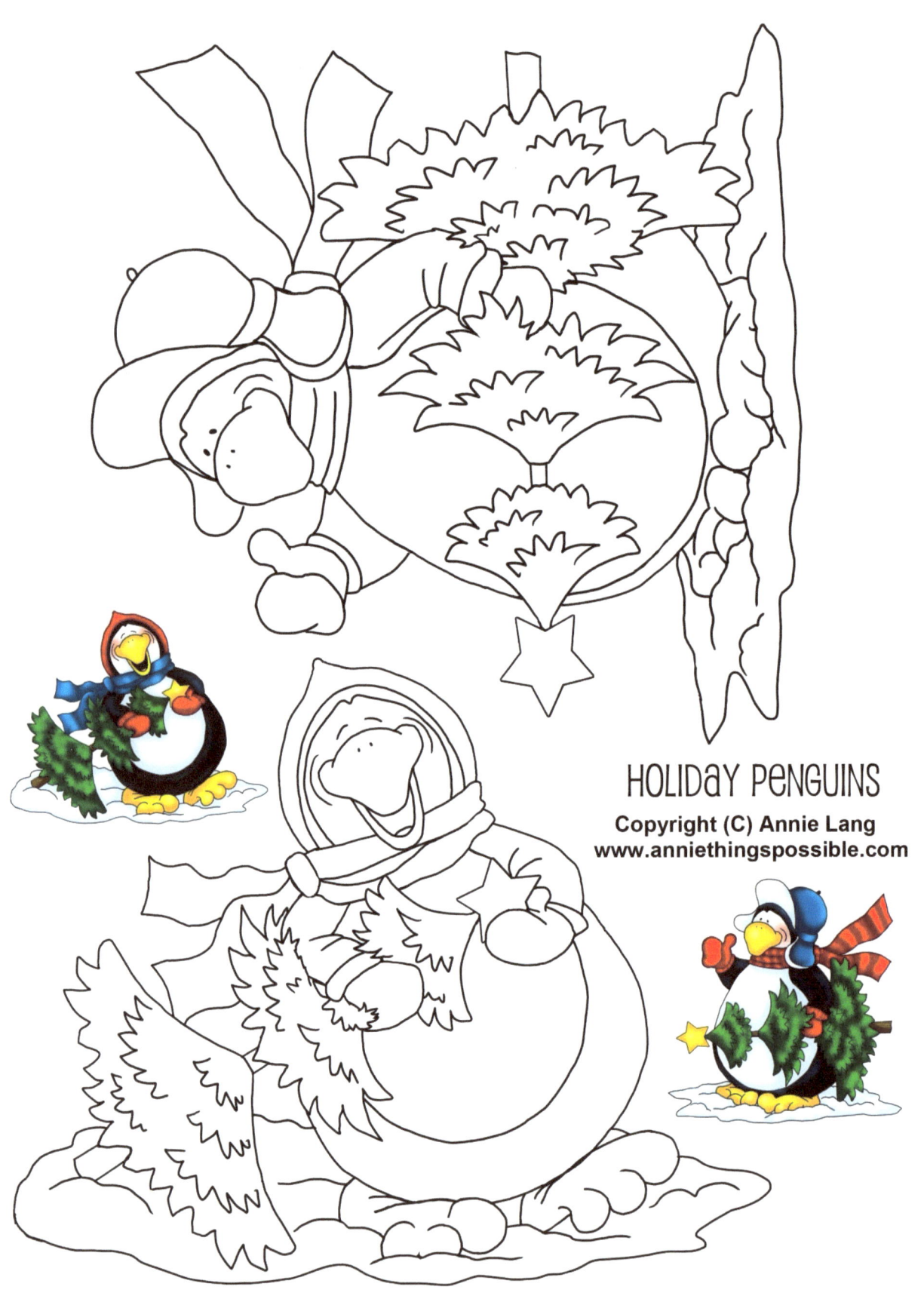

HOLIDAY PENGUINS

HOLIDAY PENGUINS

HOLIDAY PENGUINS

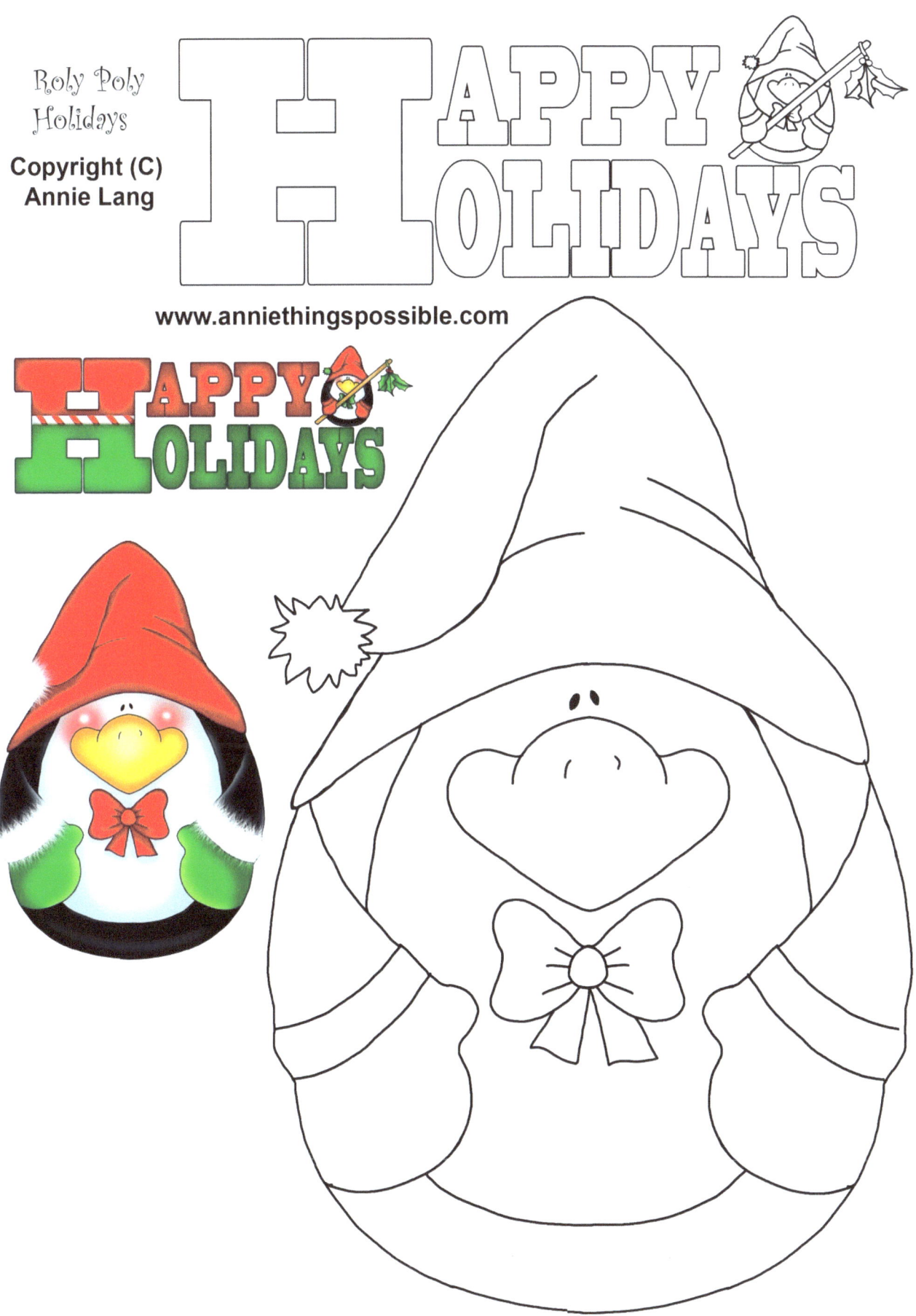

Roly Poly
Holidays

**Copyright (C)
Annie Lang**

www.anniethingspossible.com

Roly Poly Holidays

SOMETHING JUST for YOU!

SOMETHING JUST for YOU!

Roly Poly Holidays

Copyright (C) Annie Lang
www.anniethingspossible.com

Roly Poly Holidays

SEASON'S GREETINGS

SEASON'S GREETINGS

Roly Poly Holidays

Roly Poly Holidays

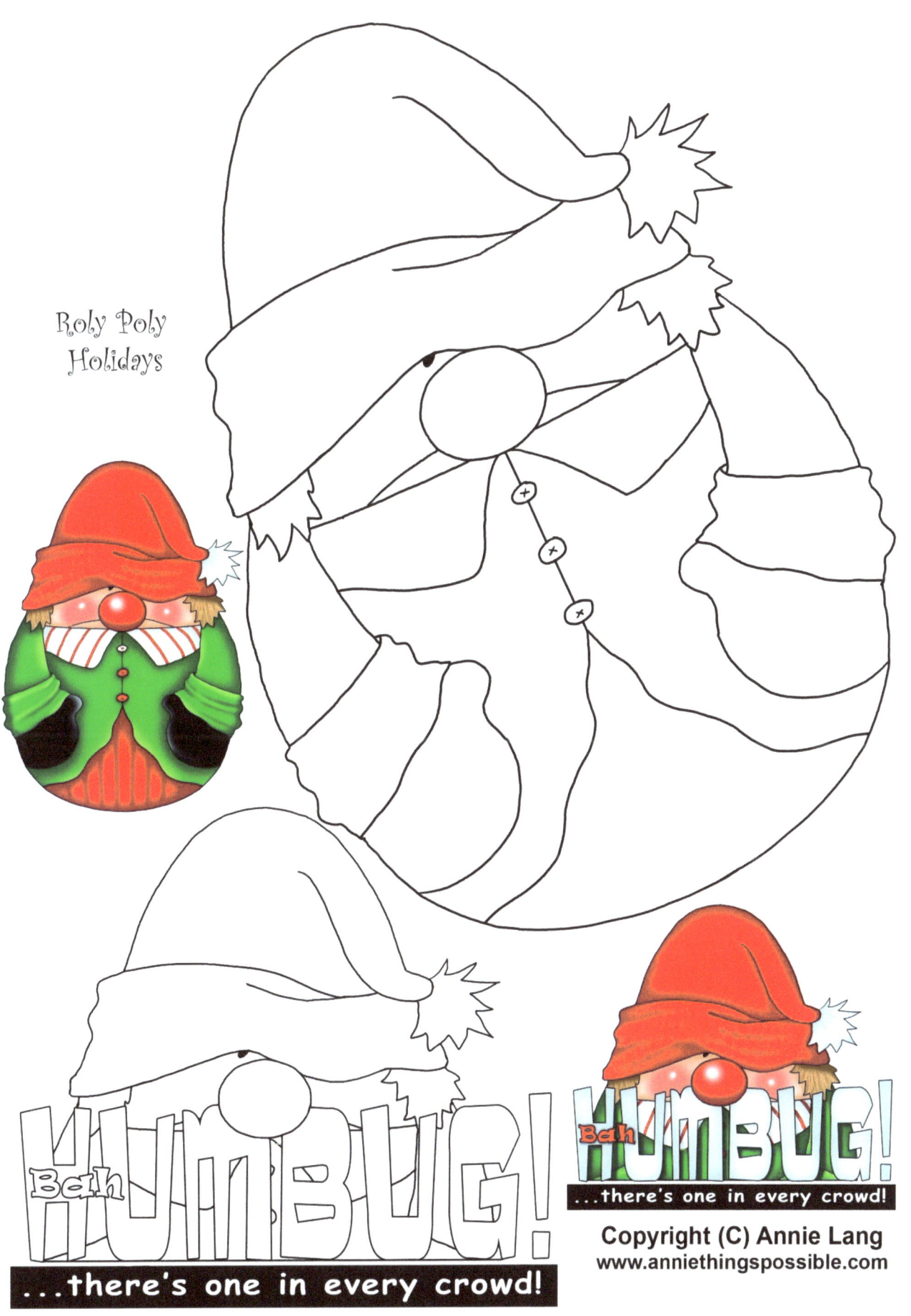

Roly Poly
Holidays

Bah HUMBUG!
...there's one in every crowd!

Bah HUMBUG!
...there's one in every crowd!

Annie's Singing
Christmas Mice

Copyright (C) Annie Lang   www.anniethingspossible.com

Copyright (C) Annie Lang
www.anniethingspossible.com

Annie's Singing Christmas Mice

Annie's Singing
Christmas Mice

Copyright (C) Annie Lang
www.anniethingspossible.com

Annie's Singing Christmas Mice

Annie's Singing Christmas Mice

Copyright (C) Annie Lang
www.anniethingspossible.com

Annie's Singing Christmas Mice

Annie's
Singing
Christmas Mice

Annie's Singing
Christmas Mice

Annie's
Singing
Christmas
Mice

Annie's
Holiday Tree
Trimmer Kids

Annie's
Bringin' Home
the Christmas
Tree Kids

Annie's
Holiday Mistletoe Kids

Copyright (C) Annie Lang
www.anniethingspossible.com

Annie's
Christmas Tree
Garland
Kids

Annie's
Christmas
Gift Girl

Copyright (C) Annie Lang
www.anniethingspossible.com

Annie's Christmas Gift Boy

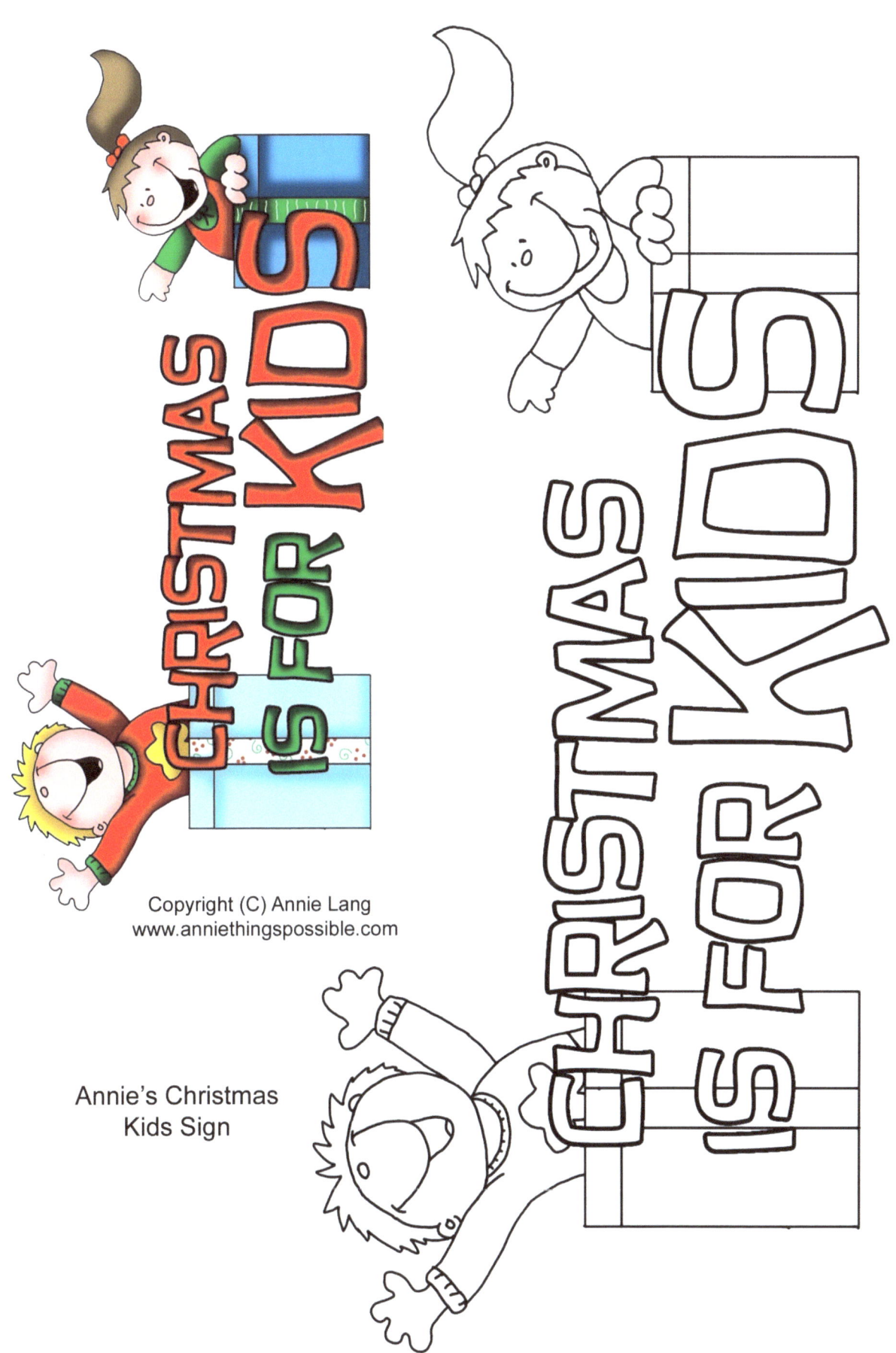

Copyright (C) Annie Lang
www.anniethingspossible.com

Annie's Christmas
Kids Sign

notes and memos

Thank you for purchasing this publication!

Find dozens of other fun titles on my
Annie Lang's Books website!

*I hope you enjoyed this book and
encourage you to leave a review and share your
thoughts for other customers at Amazon.com!*

*To learn more about the author, get free project
ideas, see video how-to's and more, please visit
Annie Lang's BLOG at
http://annielang-anniethingspossible.blogspot.com/*